A-Z of Animals

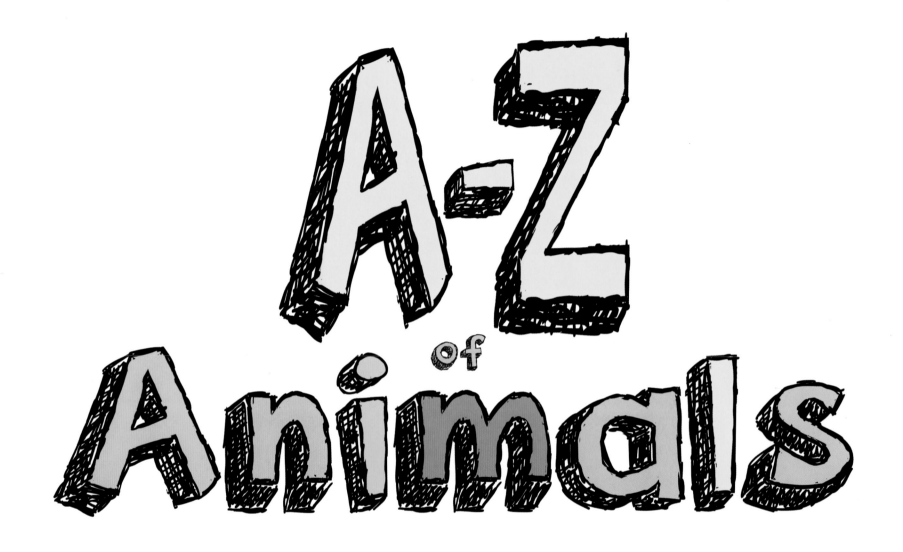

A-Z of Animals

Tom Jackson

amber
BOOKS

Published by
Amber Books Ltd
United House
North Road
London
N7 9DP
United Kingdom
www.amberbooks.co.uk
Appstore: itunes.com/apps/amberbooksltd
Facebook: www.facebook.com/amberbooks
Twitter: @amberbooks

ISBN: 978-1-78274-686-7

Project Editor: Sarah Uttridge
Design: Keren Harragan

All artworks © IMP AB apart from the following: 26 and 29 both © Amber Books Ltd

Printed in China

Contents

Aa

Alligator

Lives in swamps.

Tail
Alligators can be up to 13 feet (4 meters) from nose to tail.

Teeth
Alligators have between 74 and 80 teeth in their mouth.

Alligators are found in America and China.

Bear

Hunts in cold forests.

Brown bears can live for up to 30 years in the wild.

Fur
Bears can also have some fur that is gray, fair, or black.

Claws
If in danger, young bears use their claws to climb up trees.

Cc

Camel

Lives in deserts.

Humps
Central Asian camels have two humps. The camels from Africa and the Middle East have one.

The fat in the hump keeps the camel alive without drinking or eating for a week.

Nostrils
The camel can shut its nostrils to stop sand getting inside.

Dolphin

Lives in groups called pods.

Echo
Dolphins talk with high-pitched sounds that humans cannot hear.

Air Breather
Dolphins come to the surface to breathe through a blowhole in the top of the head.

The dolphin has no nose. It smells using its tongue.

9

Ee

Elephant

The largest land animal.

There are two kinds of elephants: African ones with large ears, like this one, and Asian ones with smaller ears.

Trunk

The trunk contains 40,000 muscles. The elephant uses the tip to feel objects.

Tusks

The tusks are long teeth used for digging and fighting.

Frog

Ff

The round sac under the mouth makes the frog's call louder.

Always lives near water.

Skin
Bright colors are used to scare off other animals.

Feet
The toes have pads on the bottom that help the frog grip when it climbs.

11

Gg

Giraffe

Eats trees in Africa.

The giraffe is the tallest animal in the world. It is as high as a two-story house.

Neck
It has the same number of bones in its neck as a human.

Babies
When a giraffe is born it is already taller than most people.

The giraffe's tongue is blue and is as long as a man's forearm.

Hippopotamus

Hh

Name means "water horse."

During the day, hippos stay cool in rivers and lakes. At night they climb onto land to eat grass.

Skin
The skin makes its own orange-colored sunscreen.

Feet
Hippos have webbed feet, with the toes linked by skin to help with swimming.

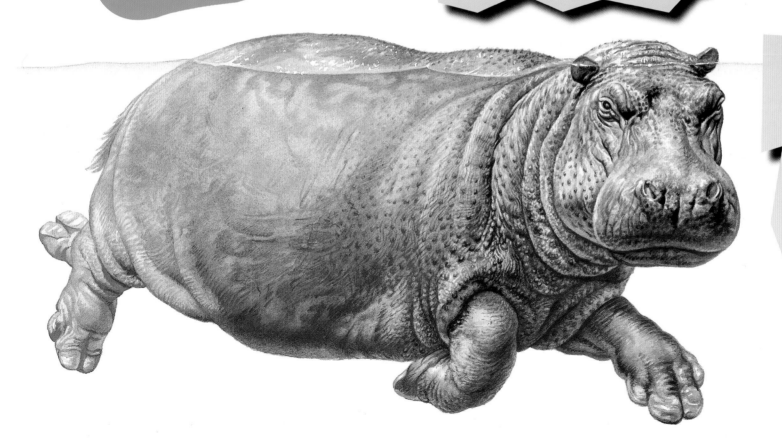

Ii

Iguana

Big American lizard.

The lizard does not have an outer ear. All that is seen is the smooth, round eardum on the side of the head.

Skin
The iguana's skin gets darker in cold weather.

Claws
Iguanas use their claws to climb in trees to eat leaves and find insects.

Jaguar

A stealthy rainforest hunter.

Rosettes

The rings of spots keep the cat hidden in the jungle shadows.

The jaguar is the only big cat to live in the Americas.

Attack

Jaguars wait on a branch for prey to pass—and then leap onto their backs.

15

Kk

Kangaroo

An Australian grass-eater.

A male kangaroo is called a jack, a female is a jill, and the baby is joey.

Hopping It

Kangaroos cannot walk but hop on their back legs, bouncing up to 33 feet (10 meters) at a time!

Pouch

Babies spend six months in a tummy pouch.

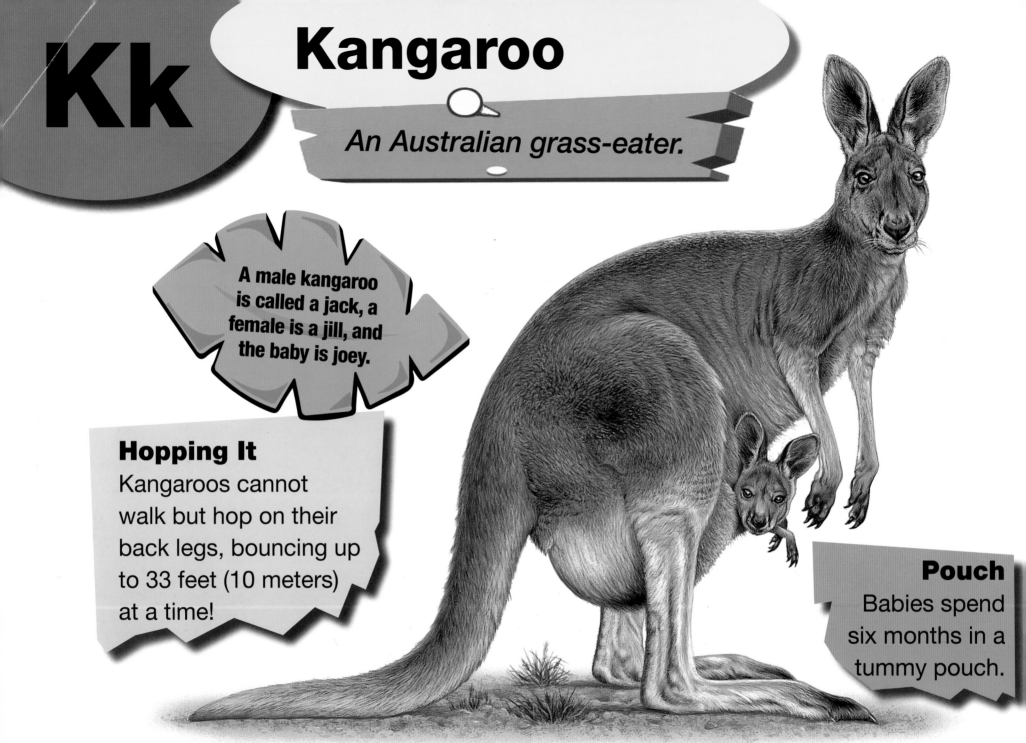

Lion

Ll

Tongue
The lion's tongue is so rough it rips meat from bones.

Hunts in teams.

Family Cat
Lions live in a family called a pride. The pride is ruled by the strongest male.

There are two kinds of lion: One from Africa, the other from India.

Mm

Monkey

Lives in rainforests.

Extra Grip
American monkeys can wrap their tails around tree branches.

There are 260 kinds of monkey living in Central and South America, Africa, and Asia.

Clever Brains
Monkeys have good memories so they do not get lost in the forest.

Narwhal

An Arctic whale.

Spiral Tooth

This whale has a long tusk. This is a giant tooth that grows through the upper lip.

The narwhal suck up shellfish from the seabed.

Unicorn

In the Middle Ages, people thought narwhal tusks were magical unicorn horns!

Narwhals dive under the ice of the frozen Arctic Ocean.

19

Oo

Octopus

A bottom-dwelling hunter.

Sharp Mouth
The octopus's only hard body part is its beak-like mouth.

The octopus moves using a jet of water blasted from a tube.

Color Trick
An octopus hides by changing color to match the seabed.

Panda

Lives in Chinese hills.

A panda goes to the toilet 50 times a day.

Smallest Babies
A newborn baby panda is 1,500 times smaller than its mother.

Bamboo
Giant pandas only eat bamboo leaves. They spend 16 hours a day eating.

A panda's wrist bones poke out to grip bamboo like having a sixth finger.

21

Queen Parrotfish

A large coral fish.

Sleeping Bag
The parrotfish sleeps inside a bubble of slime. The slime wobbles when a fish gets too close.

Beak Face
The fish scrapes food from rocks using its sharp beak-shaped teeth.

The meat of parrotfish is poisonous to humans.

Rhinoceros

Rr

A tough plant-eater.

Armor
A rhino's tough skin is as thick as 200 pieces of paper.

Hair Horn
Rhino horn is made from hairs that are joined together into a solid spike.

The word rhinoceros means "nose horn."

Ss

Shark

Hunting fish.

Big Hunter
The White Shark is the biggest hunting shark. It can swim along as fast as a speedboat.

Electricity
Sensors on the snout can pick up the movement of other animals.

Over its lifetime, a White Shark grows 3,000 teeth.

Tiger

Tt

A quiet hunter from East Asia.

Biggest Cat
Tigers from Siberia are the largest cats in the world.

Unlike house cats, tigers are strong swimmers.

Striped Disguise
The stripes help the tiger hide in tall grasses.

Unicornfish

Spiny fish from coral reefs.

Fleshy Horn

The fish's "horn" is a long bony spine that grows from the front of the skull.

Tail Spikes

Two sharp spikes point forward from either side of the base of the fish's tail.

Unicornfish eat tiny animals floating in the water.

Vulture

Vv

Eats dead bodies.

The King Vulture of South America has a wingspan of 7 feet (2 meters).

Naked Head

A vulture's bald head stops it getting messy with blood when eating dead animals.

Sniffing Food

Vultures can smell a dead animal's body from more than a mile away.

Ww

Whale

Enormous ocean animals.

Ocean Giant

The Blue Whale is the biggest animal ever. Its tongue is the size of an elephant!

The Blue Whale's heart is as big as a four-seat car.

Filter Feed

Large whales eat tiny animals. Their mouths sieve them from seawater.

X-Ray Fish

Xx

River fish from South America.

See-through
The fish's scaly skin is almost see-through so you can see inside the body like looking at an X-ray.

The fish's skin looks golden in strong sunlight.

Insect Hunter
The X-ray fish lives in shoals (groups of fish).

Yy

Yak

Mountain cow.

Big Cow
Yaks are related to farm cows, but they are larger and have thick hairs.

Wild yaks are now rare. Most yaks are tame and used for carrying heavy loads.

Up High
Yaks eat grass in the meadows of the Himalayan Mountains in Asia.

Zebra

Zz

Grassland grazer.

Stripes

Zebras live in large herds. Every animal has its own stripe pattern.

Zebras dig into dry riverbeds with their hooves to find water.

Zebras live in Africa. They are wild relatives of horses and donkeys.

Staying Safe

The stripes make it harder for a lion attacker to keep track of a zebra during a deadly chase.

31

Aa Alligator	**Hh** Hippopotamus	**Oo** Octopus	**Vv** Vulture
Bb Bear	**Ii** Iguana	**Pp** Panda	**Ww** Whale
Cc Camel	**Jj** Jaguar	**Qq** Queen Parrotfish	**Xx** X-Ray Fish
Dd Dolphin	**Kk** Kangaroo	**Rr** Rhinoceros	**Yy** Yak
Ee Elephant	**Ll** Lion	**Ss** Shark	**Zz** Zebra
Ff Frog	**Mm** Monkey	**Tt** Tiger	
Gg Giraffe	**Nn** Narwhal	**Uu** Unicornfish	